Gluten-Free

MAIN DISHES

What is Gluten?

Gluten is a protein that is found in wheat, rye, and barley. There are many reasons people avoid gluten. Some people are allergic to wheat itself while others may have a sensitivity to gluten and just feel better when they avoid it. The most serious is Celiac Disease, in which the body produces an autoimmune response after eating gluten. The only way to manage this condition is to follow a strict gluten-free diet.

No More Bread? No Pasta?

At first, going gluten-free may appear to be rather limiting. Fortunately, there are many more delicious foods on the gluten-free list than on the forbidden list. There are also more and more products, from cereals to baking mixes to pastas, which are now being formulated in gluten-free versions. These days you'll find them not just in health food stores and online, but also on the shelves of most major supermarkets.

Some Good News

Spotting hidden gluten in processed foods is a lot easier now thanks to the FDA's Food Allergy Labeling Law that went into effect in 2004. Since wheat is a common allergen, any product that contains wheat or is derived from it must say so on the label. That means formerly questionable ingredients, such as modified food starch or maltodextrin, must now show wheat as part of their name if they were made from it (for example, "wheat maltodextrin"). Be aware that this ONLY applies to foods produced in the US and Canada. Imports are a different matter.

More Good News

Look at your dietary restrictions as an opportunity to try new foods. Add quinoa and chickpea flour to your cupboard. Use corn tortillas to make sandwiches or lasagna. You'll find easy recipes in this book that are so delicious you'll forget that they're gluten-free. Healthy eating may actually be easier without gluten, too. Adding more fresh produce to your meals, eating less processed food and avoiding refined flour are all steps to a better diet for anyone.

Gluten-Free Flour Blends

While there are many products that are now readily available in the supermarkets, they can be rather expensive. We have provided a basic flour blend that can be prepared in bulk and kept on hand for use at any time. Please refer to this when preparing many of the recipes in this book.

Gluten-Free All-Purpose Flour Blend

1 cup white rice flour

1 cup sorghum flour

1 cup tapioca flour

1 cup cornstarch

1 cup almond flour or coconut flour

Combine all ingredients in large bowl. Whisk to make sure flours are evenly distributed. The recipe can be doubled or tripled. Store in airtight container in the refrigerator.

Makes about 5 cups

Neptune's Spaghetti Squash

1 **spaghetti squash (about 2 pounds)**

3 **tablespoons olive oil**

1 **clove garlic, minced**

8 **ounces medium raw shrimp (with tails on), peeled and deveined**

8 **ounces bay scallops**

1/2 **cup fresh or frozen peas**

1/4 **cup sun-dried tomatoes in oil, drained and chopped**

1/2 **teaspoon dried basil**

1/4 **cup grated Parmesan cheese**

1. Cut spaghetti squash in half lengthwise; remove seeds. Place squash, cut side down, in large microwavable dish. Cover with vented plastic wrap. Microwave on HIGH 9 minutes or until squash separates easily into strands when tested with fork.

2. Meanwhile, heat oil in large skillet over medium-high heat. Add garlic; cook and stir 1 minute. Add shrimp, scallops, peas, tomatoes and basil; cook and stir 1 to 2 minutes or until shrimp are pink and opaque and scallops are opaque.

3. Separate squash strands with fork. Divide evenly among four bowls. Top squash with seafood mixture; gently toss. Sprinkle with cheese.

Makes 4 servings

Apple-Cherry Glazed Pork Chops

1/4 to 1/2 teaspoon dried thyme

1/8 teaspoon salt

1/8 teaspoon black pepper

2 boneless pork loin chops
(about 3 ounces each),
trimmed of fat

2/3 cup unsweetened apple
juice

1/2 small apple, sliced

2 tablespoons sliced green
onion

2 tablespoons dried tart
cherries

1 tablespoon water

1 teaspoon cornstarch

1. Combine thyme, salt and pepper in small bowl. Rub onto both sides of pork chops.

2. Spray large skillet with nonstick cooking spray; heat over medium heat. Add pork chops; cook 3 to 5 minutes or until barely pink in center, turning once. Remove to plate; keep warm.

3. Add apple juice, apple slices, green onion and cherries to same skillet. Simmer 2 to 3 minutes or until apple and green onion are tender.

4. Stir water into cornstarch in small bowl until smooth; stir into skillet. Bring to a boil; cook and stir until thickened. Spoon apple mixture over pork chops.

Makes 2 servings

Bean Ragoût with Cilantro-Cornmeal Dumplings

2 cans (about 14 ounces each) diced tomatoes

1 can (about 15 ounces) pinto or kidney beans, rinsed and drained

1 can (about 15 ounces) black beans, rinsed and drained

1½ cups chopped red bell peppers

1 onion, chopped

2 zucchini, sliced

½ cup chopped green bell pepper

½ cup chopped celery

1 poblano pepper, chopped

3 tablespoons chili powder

2 teaspoons ground cumin

2 cloves garlic, minced

1 teaspoon dried oregano

¼ teaspoon salt

⅛ teaspoon black pepper

Cilantro-Cornmeal Dumplings (recipe follows)

Slow Cooker Directions

1. Combine tomatoes, beans, red bell peppers, onion, zucchini, green bell pepper, celery, poblano pepper, chili powder, cumin, garlic, oregano, salt and black pepper in slow cooker; mix well. Cover; cook on LOW 7 to 8 hours.

2. Prepare Cilantro-Cornmeal Dumplings 1 hour before serving.

3. Turn slow cooker to HIGH. Drop dumplings by level tablespoonfuls (larger dumplings will not cook properly) on top of ragoût. Cover; cook 1 hour or until toothpick inserted into dumplings comes out clean.

Makes 6 servings

Cilantro-Cornmenal Dumplings

¼ cup Gluten-Free All-Purpose Flour Blend (page 5)*

¼ cup yellow cornmeal

½ teaspoon baking powder

½ teaspoon xanthan gum

¼ teaspoon salt

1 tablespoon shortening

1 tablespoon shredded Cheddar cheese

2 teaspoons minced fresh cilantro

¼ cup milk

Or use any all-purpose gluten-free flour blend that does not contain xanthan gum.

Combine flour blend, cornmeal, baking powder, xanthan gum and salt in medium bowl; mix well. Cut in shortening with pastry blender or two knives until coarse crumbs form. Stir in cheese and cilantro. Stir in milk just until dry ingredients are moistened.

Polenta Lasagna

4¼ cups water, divided

1½ cups yellow cornmeal

4 teaspoons finely chopped fresh marjoram

2 medium red bell peppers, chopped

1 teaspoon olive oil

2 packages (8 ounces each) sliced mushrooms

1 cup chopped leeks

1 clove garlic, minced

½ cup (2 ounces) shredded part-skim mozzarella cheese

2 tablespoons chopped fresh basil

1 tablespoon chopped fresh oregano

⅛ teaspoon black pepper

4 tablespoons freshly grated Parmesan cheese, divided

1. Bring 4 cups water to a boil in medium saucepan over high heat. Slowly add cornmeal, stirring constantly. Reduce heat to low; stir in marjoram. Simmer 15 to 20 minutes or until polenta thickens and pulls away from side of pan. Spread in ungreased 13X9-inch baking pan. Cover and chill about 1 hour or until firm.

2. Preheat oven to 350°F. Spray 11X7-inch baking dish with nonstick cooking spray. Place bell peppers and remaining ¼ cup water in food processor or blender; process until smooth.

3. Heat oil in medium nonstick skillet over medium heat. Add mushrooms, leeks and garlic; cook and stir 5 minutes or until leeks are crisp-tender. Stir in mozzarella cheese, basil, oregano and black pepper.

4. Cut polenta into 12 (3½-inch) squares; arrange six squares in bottom of prepared dish. Spread with half of bell pepper mixture, half of vegetable mixture and 2 tablespoons Parmesan cheese. Top with remaining six squares of polenta, remaining bell pepper and vegetable mixtures and Parmesan cheese.

5. Bake 20 minutes or until cheese is melted and polenta is golden brown.

Makes 6 servings

Baked Penne with Sausage and Peppers

8 ounces uncooked gluten-free brown rice penne pasta

1 tablespoon olive oil

1 pound hot or mild Italian sausage, removed from casings

1 large yellow bell pepper, cut into 1/2-inch pieces

1 large green bell pepper, cut into 1/2-inch pieces

1 jar (24 ounces) gluten-free spicy tomato-basil marinara sauce

2 cups (8 ounces) shredded part-skim mozzarella cheese, divided

Chopped fresh basil (optional)

1. Preheat oven to 350°F.

2. Cook pasta according to package directions until al dente. Drain; cover and keep warm.

3. Meanwhile, heat oil in large nonstick skillet over medium heat. Add sausage; cook 5 minutes, stirring to break up meat. Add bell peppers; cook 5 to 7 minutes or until sausage is browned and bell peppers are crisp-tender. Drain fat.

4. Add marinara sauce to skillet; cook 3 minutes or until heated through. Stir in penne.

5. Spread half of penne mixture in 2-quart casserole. Top with 1 cup cheese. Layer with remaining penne mixture and 1 cup cheese.

6. Bake 25 to 30 minutes or until heated through and cheese is melted. Garnish with basil.

Makes 8 servings

Parmesan-Crusted Chicken

4 boneless skinless chicken breasts (about 4 ounces each)

$^1/_4$ cup Gluten-Free All-Purpose Flour Blend (page 5)*

$^1/_4$ cup grated Parmesan cheese

2 teaspoons Italian seasoning

$^1/_2$ teaspoon salt

$^1/_2$ teaspoon black pepper

2 tablespoons olive oil

*Or use any all-purpose gluten-free flour blend that does not contain xanthan gum.

1. Pound chicken breasts between sheets of waxed paper using meat mallet to $^1/_4$-inch thickness. Combine flour blend, cheese, Italian seasoning, salt and pepper in large resealable food storage bag.

2. Add one chicken breast to bag at a time; shake to coat evenly. Heat oil in large nonstick skillet over medium heat. Cook chicken in single layer 4 to 5 minutes per side or until golden brown and no longer pink.

Makes 4 servings

Serving Suggestion: Serve this savory dish with assorted vegetables like broccoli and carrots.

Tamale Pie

Topping

3/4 **to 1 cup gluten-free biscuit baking mix**

1/2 **cup milk**

1 **egg**

2 **tablespoons butter, melted**

1/2 **jalapeño pepper,* finely chopped**

Filling

1 **tablespoon olive oil**

1 **green bell pepper, chopped**

3/4 **cup chopped green onions**

2 **cloves garlic, finely chopped**

8 **ounces ground turkey**

1 1/2 **cups canned crushed tomatoes**

1 **can (about 15 ounces) pinto beans, rinsed and drained**

2 **teaspoons chili powder**

1 **teaspoon ground cumin**

1/4 **teaspoon black pepper**

*Jalapeño peppers can sting and irritate the skin, so wear rubber gloves when handling peppers and do not touch your eyes.

1. Preheat oven to 425°F. Spray 9-inch pie plate with nonstick cooking spray.

2. For topping, stir baking mix, milk, egg, butter and jalapeño in medium bowl until well blended;** set aside.

3. For filling, heat oil in large nonstick skillet over medium heat. Add bell pepper, green onions and garlic; cook and stir 5 minutes or until vegetables are tender. Add turkey; cook and stir until no longer pink. Add tomatoes, beans, chili powder, cumin and black pepper; cook and stir 5 minutes or until heated through.

4. Spoon vegetable mixture into prepared pie plate. Drop heaping tablespoonfuls of topping over filling.

5. Bake 25 to 30 minutes or until topping is golden brown. Let stand 5 minutes before serving.

Makes 4 servings

**The consistency of the topping will vary depending on the baking mix used in the recipe. Be sure the batter is smooth and thick. If is too thin, it will spread.

Beef and Bean Enchiladas

8 ounces ground beef

1 can (about 15 ounces) pinto beans, rinsed and drained

1/2 teaspoon ground cumin

1/2 teaspoon salt, divided

1/4 teaspoon black pepper, divided

1 tablespoon canola oil

1 onion, chopped

1 green bell pepper, chopped

1 jalapeño pepper,* minced (optional)

1 clove garlic, minced

1 can (about 14 ounces) crushed tomatoes

1 1/2 teaspoons chili powder

8 (5-inch) corn tortillas, warmed

Jalapeño peppers can sting and irritate the skin, so wear rubber gloves when handling peppers and do not touch your eyes.

1. Preheat oven to 350°F. Brown beef 6 to 8 minutes in large skillet over medium-high heat, stirring to break up meat. Drain fat.

2. Mash beans in large bowl. Stir in cumin, 1/4 teaspoon salt and 1/8 teaspoon black pepper. Add beef; mix well.

3. Heat oil in same skillet over medium heat. Add onion, bell pepper, jalapeño, if desired, and garlic; cook and stir 8 to 10 minutes or until onion is translucent.

4. Stir tomatoes, chili powder, remaining 1/4 teaspoon salt and 1/8 teaspoon black pepper into skillet. Reduce heat to low; simmer 5 minutes.

5. To assemble enchiladas, spoon 1/4 cup bean mixture down center of each tortilla. Fold ends to center to enclose filling. Place in 9-inch square baking dish. Top evenly with tomato sauce.

6. Bake 20 minutes or until heated through.

Makes 4 servings

Serving Suggestion: Serve with rice and a fresh green salad.

Vegetarian Paella

2 teaspoons canola oil

1 cup chopped onion

2 cloves garlic, minced

1 cup uncooked brown rice

2¼ cups gluten-free vegetable broth

1 can (about 14 ounces) stewed tomatoes

1 small zucchini, cut into ½-inch pieces

1 cup chopped red bell pepper

1 cup coarsely chopped carrots

2 teaspoons Italian seasoning

½ teaspoon ground turmeric

⅛ teaspoon ground red pepper

1 can (14 ounces) quartered artichoke hearts, drained

½ cup frozen baby peas

¾ teaspoon salt

Slow Cooker Directions

1. Heat oil in small nonstick skillet over medium-high heat. Add onion; cook and stir 6 to 7 minutes or until tender. Stir in garlic. Transfer to slow cooker. Stir in rice.

2. Add broth, tomatoes, zucchini, bell pepper, carrots, Italian seasoning, turmeric and ground red pepper; mix well. Cover; cook on LOW 4 hours or on HIGH 2 hours or until liquid is absorbed.

3. Stir in artichokes, peas and salt. Cover; cook 5 to 10 minutes or until vegetables are tender.

Makes 6 servings

Creamy Cheese and Macaroni

1$^1/_2$ **cups uncooked gluten-free elbow macaroni**

1 **cup chopped onion**

1 **cup chopped red or green bell pepper**

$^3/_4$ **cup chopped celery**

1 **cup low-fat (1%) cottage cheese**

1 **cup (4 ounces) shredded Swiss cheese**

2 **ounces pasteurized process cheese product, cubed**

$^1/_2$ **cup whole milk**

3 **egg whites**

3 **tablespoons white rice flour**

1 **tablespoon butter**

$^1/_4$ **teaspoon black pepper**

$^1/_4$ **teaspoon gluten-free hot pepper sauce**

1. Preheat oven to 350°F. Spray 2-quart casserole with nonstick cooking spray.

2. Prepare macaroni according to package directions. Add onion, bell pepper and celery during last 5 minutes of cooking. Drain macaroni and vegetables.

3. Combine cottage cheese, Swiss cheese, cheese product, milk, egg whites, rice flour, butter, black pepper and hot pepper sauce in food processor or blender; process until smooth. Stir cheese mixture into macaroni and vegetables. Pour mixture into prepared casserole.

4. Bake 35 to 40 minutes or until golden brown. Let stand 10 minutes before serving.

Makes 6 to 8 servings

Orange Chicken Stir-Fry over Quinoa

¹/₂ **cup uncooked quinoa**

1 **cup water**

¹/₈ **teaspoon salt**

2 **teaspoons vegetable oil, divided**

1 **pound boneless skinless chicken breasts, cut into thin strips**

1 **cup fresh squeezed orange juice (2 to 3 oranges)**

1 **tablespoon gluten-free soy sauce**

1 **tablespoon cornstarch**

¹/₂ **cup sliced green onions**

2 **tablespoons grated fresh ginger**

6 **ounces snow peas, ends trimmed**

1 **cup thinly sliced carrots**

¹/₄ **teaspoon red pepper flakes (optional)**

1. Place quinoa in fine-mesh strainer; rinse well under cold running water. Bring 1 cup water to a boil in medium saucepan; stir in quinoa. Reduce heat to low; cover and simmer 10 to 15 minutes or until quinoa is tender and water is absorbed. Stir in salt.

2. Meanwhile, heat 1 teaspoon oil in large skillet over medium-high heat. Add chicken; cook 2 to 3 minutes per side or until no longer pink. Remove to plate; keep warm.

3. Stir orange juice and soy sauce into cornstarch in small bowl until smooth; set aside.

4. Heat remaining 1 teaspoon oil in skillet. Add green onions and ginger; stir-fry 1 to 2 minutes. Add snow peas and carrots; stir-fry 4 to 5 minutes or until carrots are crisp-tender.

5. Return chicken to skillet. Stir orange juice mixture; add to skillet. Bring to a boil. Reduce heat; simmer until slightly thickened.

6. Serve chicken and vegetables over quinoa; sprinkle with red pepper flakes, if desired.

Makes 4 servings

Eggplant Parmesan

2 egg whites

2 tablespoons water

1/2 cup crushed gluten-free rice cereal squares

1/4 cup plus 2 tablespoons grated Parmesan cheese, divided

1 teaspoon Italian seasoning

1 large eggplant, peeled and cut into 12 slices (about 1/2 inch thick)

2 teaspoons olive oil

1 small onion, diced

1 clove garlic, minced

2 cans (about 14 ounces each) diced tomatoes

1/2 teaspoon dried basil

1/2 teaspoon dried oregano

1/2 cup (2 ounces) shredded mozzarella cheese

1. Preheat oven to 350°F. Spray 15X10-inch jelly-roll pan with nonstick cooking spray.

2. Whisk egg whites and water in shallow dish. Combine crushed cereal, 2 tablespoons Parmesan cheese and Italian seasoning in another shallow dish. Dip eggplant slices in egg white mixture, letting excess drip back into dish. Coat in cereal mixture, pressing lightly to adhere. Place in single layer in prepared pan.

3. Bake 25 to 30 minutes or until bottoms are browned. Turn slices over; bake 15 to 20 minutes or until well browned and tender.

4. Meanwhile, heat oil in medium nonstick skillet over medium-high heat. Add onion; cook and stir 5 minutes or until softened. Add garlic; cook and stir 1 minute. Stir in tomatoes, basil and oregano; bring to a boil. Reduce heat to low; simmer 15 to 20 minutes or until sauce is thickened, stirring occasionally.

5. Spray 13X9-inch baking dish with nonstick cooking spray. Spread sauce in prepared dish. Arrange eggplant slices in single layer on top of sauce. Sprinkle with mozzarella cheese and remaining 1/4 cup Parmesan cheese.

6. Bake 15 to 20 minutes or until sauce is bubbly and cheeses are melted.

Makes 4 servings

Salmon with Brown Rice and Vegetables

- 2 **cups water**
- 12 **ounces skinless salmon fillets**
- 2 **cups sliced asparagus (1-inch pieces)**
- 2 **cups cooked brown rice**
- 1 **cup coarsely chopped fresh spinach**
- $1/3$ **cup gluten-free chicken broth**
- 2 **tablespoons chopped fresh chives**
- 2 **tablespoons lemon juice**
- $1/8$ **teaspoon black pepper**

1. Bring water to a boil in large skillet over high heat. Add salmon; reduce heat to medium-low. Cover and simmer 10 minutes or until salmon begins to flake when tested with fork. Remove salmon from skillet; cut into large pieces when cool enough to handle.

2. Spray separate large skillet with nonstick cooking spray; heat over medium-high heat. Add asparagus; cook and stir 6 minutes or until tender. Stir in rice, spinach and broth; reduce heat to low. Cover and cook 1 to 2 minutes or until spinach is wilted and rice is heated through. Stir in salmon, chives, lemon juice and pepper.

Makes 4 servings